LIFE: the poem in 3-D

we all crawl
out of the slow
dank dark
humid hole
of an other
into the bright
screaming light
of life
attached to the ewe
goo mass & marrow
of bodies
these porous vessels
of pleasure & pain
sailing nowhere
but O—
the hypercolor horizons

PAIN

THE BOARD GAME

Also by Sampson Starkweather:

Until the Joy of Death 💀 *Hits*, Spork Press, 2015

Human Week, Tungsten Press, 2015

Flux Capacitor, Black Cake Records, 2014

Flowers of Rad, Factory Hollow Press, 2014

The First Four Books of Sampson Starkweather,
Birds, LLC, 2013

Like Clouds Never Render, O'Clock Press, 2012

Self Help Poems, Greying Ghost Press, 2010

The Heart is Green from So Much Waiting,
Immaculate Disciples Press, 2010

City of Moths, Rope-a-Dope Press, 2008

The Photograph, Horse Less Press, 2007

PAIN
THE BOARD GAME

SAMPSON STARKWEATHER

password: pipedream!

 For information: Third Man Books, LLC, 623 7th Ave S, Nashville, Tennessee 37203.

Printed in Nashville, Tennessee

Library of Congress Control Number: 2015947920

FIRST EDITION
Design by Ryon Nishimori
Illustrations by Jon-Michael Frank

ISBN 978-0-9913361-2-8

CONTENTS

I. Pain Poems

II. The Plays: An Interlude

III. Human Week

IV. Until the Joy of Death Hits

PAIN POEMS

anyway, the diamond 💎 confessed

I was going to start with the stars
but didn't want to lose you
the real batons
of the metaphysical poem-police
poised to thwack
at sentimentality
the tiny trust of starting
a poem is something
I'm banking on
you down?
now now now
the arrow within
is knee-deep
I'm not asking
you to pull it out
just participate or rather
listen to me
moan
a bit
for free
economy-
less
surrender
does it matter
to what
the debris
of me
this heart-crumpled-paper
glitter
inside the surgery
my body torn
like a painting of blue
without value
the memory
of a Michael Jordan poster
in a gold chain
paused in a dream
flies from my chest
like a loosed dove

from an unknown ceremony
maybe
PAIN:
the board game
is how I'll get rich
the longed for
is a black taxi
forever driving away
an emoji
that could stand
for anything
I call you
crashed-into
because
we are all leveled
at some point
by the word
love
why fight it
the stars are a lie
which is why
whatever
but still
I'd like to see
inside one
I imagine
it's light
pouring out
warm
freakish
putting it on
like a coat
or laying it down
over a puddle
or threshold
to walk across
but I know
it is dark
and cold
and hard
in there
it is

like me
already
dead

THE STARS ARE
A LIE

blank VHS tapes

I've always wanted
a child
to name Tumult
she would wander
off into fields
cursed with courage
the way we wander
into cities
jobs loves friends
debt
that unreal river
but would always
come back
a little changed
a little less
her name
until
she didn't
...
like her daddy
who too
was never
born

self-preservation

they don't make dildos like they used to
I remember my mom's 80s vibrator
a wand with a mechanical advantage
something stolen from a sci-fi set
we pretended was a microphone 🎤
little invisible madonnas
stars shining even after they're gone
plugged it in and felt it vibrate
like the earth beneath our feet
humming its little ditty
of course its song is gone
like most things
and the memory of them
but here we are
in the elegy
of a vibrator
leveled by facts
moms masturbate
and die
and so do we
and happiness
will always be
a mystery

letter of resignation

so long language

thank you for the opportunity
you look sweet on my CV
my time here has taught me
your world is not for me

this place creates
a silent violence

spiritual detritus
the world's last light
spilling from this shipwrecked tanker

what do you think the last human dream will be

I think it might be me
jumping out the goddamn window
        yelling
who's coming with me!

good luck steam cleaning the semen

sincerely

poetry

SO LONG LANGUAGE

I don't know how to pray

so I watch amateur porn
from the 80s
the performers glow
but I know
they are currently dead
and feeling more alive
I come
like god
~~~~~~~~~
~~~~~~~~~
~~~~~~~~~

100,000 alone
~~~~~~~~~

poem

oops, I did it again

3 shots to the chest at the arcade

Sadness is my favorite video game
I am its hero
the little man with facial hair
scampering through pixilated cities
looking for clues
and accumulating shit
without knowing why
trying not
to be crushed
or free fall
into the not-world's dark
as 8-bit clouds
scroll across the pre-
programmed sky
it's exhausting
but I take it
next level
I am happy here
it feels real
and I can always die

SADNESS IS MY FAVORITE VIDEO GAME

I am often associated with flowers

Hello, my name is Charles Baudelaire.

I was born in 1976, where I was raised in Pittsboro, North Carolina.

I am a poet. It says so on my Wikipedia page.

My themes are beauty in the modern world, the fleeting, ephemeral experience of life in the age of the internet and Mac products, and the responsibility art has to capture that experience.

My first 4 books went mostly ignored and was soon forgotten, although it is still available on e-Bay for $22.84.

Tiny cookies of my life are crumbled around the internet, most notably a nude photo covered in chapbooks, that too will be buried.

I am poor, ADD, drunk, and might be masturbating to death.

I am this close to moving back in with my mother, or at least "renting" her house on Airbnb while she vacations in Mexico.

I will probably die of syphilis... again.

No one will leave flowers at my grave.

The End.

how to enjoy your new ghost

the first thing you'll notice
when you tear open
the packaging
is your ghost
is just like you
(white and bound
to disappoint)
imagine everything
you've ever lost
love ♥ money 💵 people 🚶 👩
opportunities 🚪 time ⌛
memories 💭 blah blah blah
all repackaged
and marketed to you
and your customized damage
finally you have something
you can't lose
for best results
you should die
💀
now lie back
and watch
your ghost
go
👻

letters to a young rapper

this poetry game
used to think
shorties be like
uummmmmm, poetry
but they be like
eewwwwwww, poetry
and I be like
alone

attention deficit disorder

I'm struggling
to focus
like a hand-held
home-movie
of a dead
loved one
in the woods
naked in front
of a waterfall
doing something
impossible
to describe
all true ghosts
go straight to
VHS
this is the point
in the poem
where it must decide
between
love or death
hmmmm
who didn't crush
on a shy gangly
employee
of a video store
renting
Wild @ Heart
religiously
as a message
remember love
is the shit
and nobody
has to die
in a poem
at this time
I'd like to invite
Nicholas Cage up
to the stage
SPOILER ALERT
love
& snakeskin
win

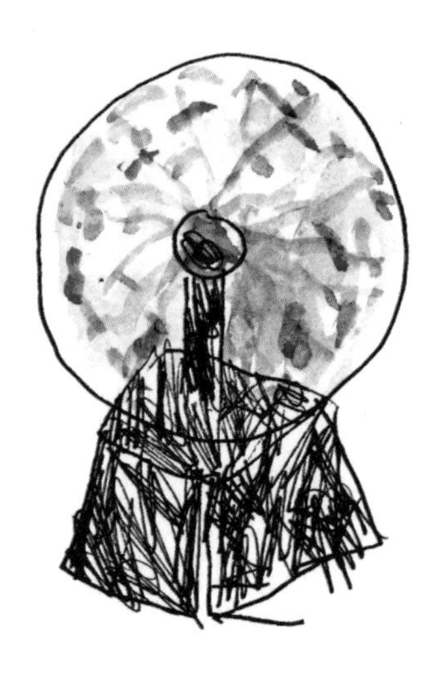

LOVE IS THE
SHIT

cutting off your penis is like suicide for pussies

the revolving wow
of being alive
1994
driving drunk
through the tree
of now
the want
to know
a fatalistic
desire
face it
I will die
inside
a pixilated pussy
like reverse déjà vu
this is always
already
not happening
my face frozen
on a conference call
with the future
this is Shame speaking:
abandon the poem
destroy all love
and its allegiances
end this suffering now
just a little boy
with a cheat code
for pain
scanning
the hard-drives
of the dead
Control-Alt-Delete
the debris
of being
nothing
to retain
except shame
is the secret
of the world

March sadness

all four
#1 seeds
have advanced
in the broken
bracket
of my heart:
]–Depression Fear–[
vs]– –[vs
]–Anxiety Shame–[
my team
colors
are white
guilt
you'll find me
face down
drown
in this office
pool
the crowd
going
wild
at my
demise

dear shareholders

I work
pro bono
(for tax purposes)
"being alive"
is my office
@ work
I only shit
on the 9th floor
as a matter
of spiritual principle
my dream
is the star
of a snuff film
the world
is shit
and piss
and dis-
appointment
& misery
& helplessness
& suffering
& pain
& fear
& death
please hold
the elevator

THE WORLD IS SHIT AND PISS AND DIS-APPOINTMENT

why I'm firing the agent of my YA novel adaptation of Dante's Inferno

illegibility of existence
is thrilling
like handwriting
of the recently
deceased
wells like life
offer a notness
to fill in
sing or swim
the moral of
any story
is music
ashes, ashes
we all fall down
pretty much
sums it up
this endless
not knowing
or existing
...NOT!
get it
grave-diggers
are running
out of room or so says
Gravedigger Magazine
and look
like a floweringaxe
the ground opens
one-thousand-mouthed
for you
who, platitude-ed
rock-bottomed
here at last
in the ill-prepared id
crawl out
of your self
forever
for what
you're promised
is a helluva view

I used to cheat @ Candyland when I was a child

dat death-flavored
Blow Pop™
tho
lick it
'til you get
to the gum
blow a big black
bubble
when it POPs
the poem is over
we are all
lost
in the licorice
forest

stuck between The Rock and late capitalism

we all
must choose
the wall
or the wave
my uncle
chose both
teaching me
how to drown
with grace
which I equate
with 80s wrestlers
a beautiful
uselessness
nightmares
are just dreams
that come true
we are all
in the same
documentary
but you can't Netflix
Death™
just yet

NO DREAMS COME TRUE

gay bar

you are all my children
I'm drunk
off privilege
a shoo-in
for an Oscar
as the other
other
my astrological sign
is antimatter
I live for the funk
I die for the funk
my health insurance
is called patience™
I just wait
like a run-over dog
in the rain
letting nature do
what it do
I don't procreate
I martyrbate
Jesus-esque
you could say
I'm full
of passionate
apathy
sometimes I breathe
(without even thinking about it)
and yes
I forgive myself
for whatever
happens
next

post-police rainbow

angels fall
for like...
ever
I don't know
how to say this
but there's a darkness
that allows
for truly miraculous shit to shine
revelatory to the depth
beneath the depth
anti-double-rainbowed
only underground
where you sit
poised at a piano
too beautiful
militant as fuck
trolling eternity
where rhetoric and music meet
a kind of diamond 💎 forms
singing for no reason
which is the reason
the heart commands
there is no such thing
as not-language
a rote desire
and certain nostalgia
that comes
from any anachronistic existence
as for me?
I poured my 40 oz out
in the forest for you
did a weird dance
with the unwilling trees
dreamed you bathing
in black flowers
floating like a bear above the ether
but I know right–
who cares?
this is just a poem...
what I'm trying to say is
fuck angels
you have friends

find & replace

replace god with fear
a real religion
the infinite annihilation
of hope for as long as language has allowed
a rope coming to an end
my b on being so real
but I'm talking about the end
of the world
not the cool kind with fire and zombies
or a hero or heroine
walking around dystopian cityscapes
searching for gasoline or meaning or humanity
or something to rescue
but another apocalypse
which is already here
unfolding over and over
like waves
crashing at the feet of no savior
I mean the dream
of standing on a beach
in front of a huge blue tsunami
and you turn to find a towering wall—
the true formlessness of life
letting itself be known
we see the world end so many times
our soul is a polaroid
in reverse
obscuring to a blankness
vivid in its notness
memory never stood
a chance
lying in the grass
with you
in the park
at night
under the stars
a slow kiss
all of this
comes
finally
to an end
I'm afraid

REPLACE GOD WITH FEAR A REAL RELIGION

nothing was the first erasure

I want
to write
a novel
of light
protagonist
of limitless
particles
points &
waves
she will speak
like me
naturally
which is to say
appropriated
from you
like poetry
she ends
infinitely
and fucks a bit
with deconstruction
she breathes
(which I describe
at length
on pg. 52)
light is all like
today I will blaze
on this page
and obliterate
its text
obviously
she leaves
the poem
alone
...
hello
darkness
take us
home

you're so vain, you probably think this poem is about you

there is no pain
in the shower
when I sing
sometimes
I'm chill
as a president
from the future
some times
I pine
like fuck
your initials
carved
into
the tree
of me

Satan is an angel too

you can own my soul
but I will always have
this **Admin as Fuck**
ab tattoo
Xeroxing is as close
as I come
to actual light
anything
holy
at least darkness is still
something
I am a good american
I believe in the angel
of absence
I suck
at my job
technically
my title
is "Slave
of the Desire
To Be"

I SUCK AT MY JOB

I am of my times and you screengrab out of ancient nowhere

the ecstasy
of indifference
got me
glowing
my byline
defines defloweredhope
co-translator of time
that sexless text
(knifebrail)
you are
my dress
you sing
when I walk
no need
to translate that
palpable ghost
you give off glints
of fresh manifest
baby
you bare me
but barely
there are
no things
left
to love
except
for words
my songs
bring people
t
o g

ether

anti-anthem

what do we want? nothing!
when do we want it? never!

**dancing in a gold chain and white fur coat
with no shirt and championship chest hair**

'cause I ain't dead
yet mutha fuckas
don't need money
to shine
with a 💎 glamour
stemming from the desire
for glamour
thereby residing
outside of capital
or rather
floating above it
like a chandelier
of shimmering antimatter
took up the mortgage
in other words
on my own vision
meanwhile
people are dying (us)
I am fat (me)
New York gotta poet
depressed (us)
in protest
and radiating desire
we dance
in kitchens
with friends
inventing a secret
glamour
that I'm pretty
sure
saves us
this seems
like a good time
to end
a poem
love
is only
and always
beautiful

I AIN'T DEAD
YET MUTHA
FUCKAS

life noir

my death
my pet-name-here
my favorite treadmill
my imagined motorcycle
after insurance
after money taxes sex
after algorithms
beyond search engines
social media
beyond data
or clouds
beyond the limitless
after all else
has fallen away
you, like the downest boo
got my back
like a metaphysical
team of lawyers
I hold you
inconsolable
like a trophy
or a child
my death
my domestic mess
I kiss you
on the neck
and the rest
is a whirr
of there-are-no-words-for
life
my mistress
awash in whorish
othertime
alone
in the kitchen
in the dark
waiting for me
to come home
with death
on my breath

memoir

I was never born
in 1976
"never" figures
heavily in the next
few thousand pages
The Pain of Existence
is relatively nothing
compared to The Pain
of Unexistence
antimatter
the hero
of the story
and poverty
duh
helpless
as a leaf
born on the branch
of nothing
bright green
aging yellow
& why
through time
basically a genius
of failing & falling
to the ground
colorless and cracked
swept away
by wind
or whatever
the memoir ends
as I walk
through the valley
of the shadow
of minor
inconvenience

legalese, baby, legalese

language is not
to be
trusted
floating ocean
sky beach
fuckhole of snow
I want
to say
so I do
wounded with flowers
I crawl
from the $ store
to the hovel
I pay 1700 a month for
to die in
comfortably
surrounded by
bright & broken
things
I have collected
(a mute protest
against death)
a spiritual ritual
practiced by
the miserable animals
of this period
otherwise known
as
now

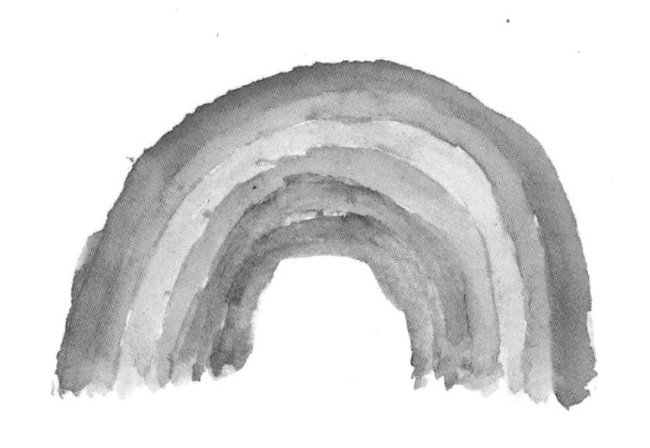

A MUTE PROTEST AGAINST DEATH

like a tiny dog running around the wreckage on the news after a tornado

a cloud of axes
descends...
sure, like a nude
on a staircase
as if it ever matters How
description is the enemy
of poetry
a perfectly suspended wave
of Whys
like that art history emoji
about-to-break
is the state
art craves
a public pain
predicated on a concealed
realness: (your knowledge here)
why go on...
why not
you sea
of question marks
no wave
(break)
?
? ?
? ?
? ?
? ?
? ?
? ?
? ?
? ?

my epitaph: fuck 🌺🌻🌹🌸🌷🌻🌹 leave 💵💰💸💵$

downloading Joy
with the world's
shittiest bandwidth
history is just god
's GIF
I've seen the future–
and it's silver
pubes
I won't hurt you
...
psych!
says the world
to absolutely nobody
before it
pummels
us all
roughly 6 feet
into the cold
perfect earth

the elusive John Cusack emoji

you have yourself
surrounded
with swimming pools
of lack
what we have
here is
some art shit
speed is seductive
yes
but slow
is oooooooooo
which is cool
'cause we suck
on each other
for (dear) life
understanding
is a mountain
and you are you
somehow
you manage
to channel a video
of a bewildered
baby goat
on a cliff face
finding a way
or me
right outside
your life
in a trench coat
holding up
a boombox

life event

I tried
to interview myself
but it's hard
to transcribe crying
besides who needs
another white dude's
mumblecore dreams
I am terrible
with Excel
spreadsheets of peace
consume me
the soul
the sole
contestant
of the ache sweepstakes
so I hoard the spoils
kick back
do some laps
in the black
swimming pool
of my fuck ups
heated to perfection
by these jets
of living-death
conveniently recorded
on my timeline

THE BLACK SWIMMING POOL OF MY FUCK UPS

goth kids on the golf course

I Shazamed
your orgasm
which found a match
in a Prince song
that didn't exist
until that exact moment
you're welcome world
sometimes I swell
with a weird mix
of nostalgia & mischievousness
thinking about
our matching
toothbrushes
writhing with electricity
instruments of
intimacy
like we're in a band
called Secret Pain
and you are the drummer
and me a roadie
with ridiculous dreams
no ideas
but in sings
see even my sadness
has steez
like a peacock
lost
on a golf course
at dusk
pining for
the rush
and famished ache
the rough magic
of bodies
illuminating
the lack
of any
limitation
when one

sex poem (if you're alive to read this)

death is a cheerleader
whose team is 0-43
so long, dream
meaning is relative
(mother/father/sister/lawyer)
or rather
a construct
a child
abandoned
at a mall
of only ideas
we are not free
fear is
a mountain formed
from all that is not
let go
let go
this poem
is pointless
there are simpler ways
to get
inside you

admin aria 📻🎼

we the poor
(I-cited) army of infinite nothing
entrenched in
the meh-struggle
the quasi-insured
Gap®-gowned ghosts
👖👗👻
frivolity-churned
turn to
hope or cope
(paper or vapor)
time-gnawed
indebted
to the buy-in
of the lie
of an or in labor
small intestine of capitalism
bleeding spleen of the government
we the invisible artists
of the people
march
somnambulantly
nowhere
week-daily
songless
art-martyrs
to die
intermittently
dreamward
in ergonomic chairs
quietly
taking it

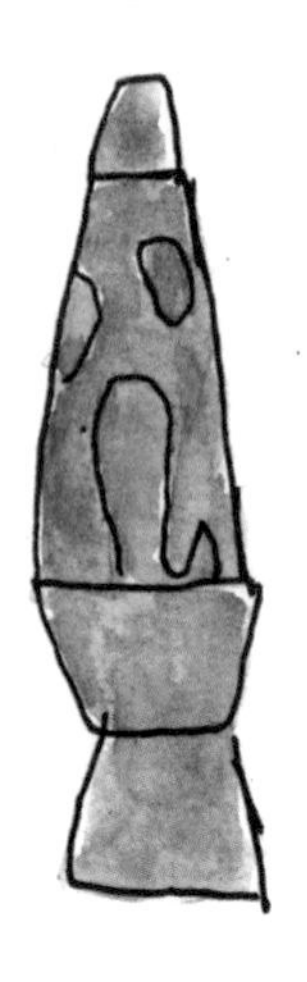

ENTRENCHED IN THE MEH-STRUGGLE

notions of the other

consume me
I'm reminded
of the time
I buried
a paperback of *The Waves*
in the backyard
itself an attempt
to bloom
not a novel
but a tree
of consciousness
from which falls
the leaves
the flowers
the betweens
diseased
diligently
gathered
to present
to no one
to the self
that shadlowlesssun

what if we call this Tenderness

some corporation
or collection agency
calls me
3 or 4 times
a day
maybe they are kind
of another mother
or ex-lover
genderless
& savagely patient
either way
they are after me
I'm convinced
they want
my poetry
I take it
wizard-level
at dodging
incoming calls
go invisible
at the grocery store
pretend
to live
in a world
without
money
my answer
ing machine
is me crying
(in French, oui)
call me
914-573-9721
please
leave me
something
tender

PRETEND TO LIVE IN
A WORLD WITHOUT
MONEY

minimum wage

grew up
dealing drugs
now poems
this is called
capital loss
no one
clicks on
this live
webcam
of my mind
(I logged off
ages ago)
the suicide
sonnets
were a flop
ditto
baby names
for clouds
Catfacebook
poetsextingatreadings.gov
spoiler alert
IT-guys shall
inherit the earth
I receive
the saddest faxes
what is grace?
what are the forms?
what is the dreamer's
responsibility
to the dream?
I'll never be
a DILF

Knight Rider ringtone

annihilated light
expectant thangs
flowers die🥀 💀
that's what flowers do
a charred swan
in a kiddy pool
is my mascot
the Fisher-Price king
of pretend™
the only thing
that makes me feel
free
is poetry
I hate people
who can afford
to live out
their dreams
suicide is the OG
#nofilter
singing in
the anvil rain
the LeBron James
of deathhacks
hard to get
more gone
oh I'll show you
how to drown
like a pro
aint no
red light
going to get us
out of this
a cellphone
at the bottom
of the ocean
blowing up

your love is like throwing ten thousand $1 bills out of a helicopter over the outfield of a minor league baseball game full of drunk mulleted spectators

baby
abort me
do I have
placenta
in my teeth
I sigh
and go viral
boredom leaked
like a plant-life
sex tape
pay attention
to the rules
Player 1 should bleed
a lot
that's pretty
much the game
see me
doggie paddle
through
the slobbered genitalia
of god
craving
a cave
to seek
refuge in
from a green wave of
(I didn't say love)
R u proud
death was all
the rage
I lived
in you

LIFE, the poem (available on blu-ray)

the goddamn ocean
suck it internet
1-800 LIFE!!
the stuff
of country music
warm rain
morning wood
the world's
stickiest sticky buns
(those things together!)
motherhood maidenhead
cantaloupe any loupe
candy candy candy 🍬
it, this, light
finite
twilight
act now
and it even
sings
🎤

SUCK IT
INTERNET

analog song

my identity
politics are
I don't exist
scroll
scroll
false archive
of affect
and swan-sex
scroll
scroll
the lives
of other
people (ha ha)
scroll
scroll
the troubling line
between breathing
and trembling
scroll
scroll
celebrity police
put bullets
in your son
scroll
scroll
place
a baby monitor
in your lungs
scroll
scroll
nostalgic for a self
still capable
of giving
a fuck
scroll
scroll
dear dark
we bare
whiteness

scroll
scroll
pity the stars
the great weight
of light
scroll
scroll
trolling time
we die
then keep dying
scroll
scroll

THE PLAYS: AN INTERLUDE

Life Without Devices

A One-act Play for Your Face

Sunlight: (speaks inaudibly)

The End.

Time & Space

Time: Hey, Space...

Space: Yes, Time...

Time: ...there is something I've been meaning to tell you...

Space: What is it?

Time: I have a crush on you.

Space: I have a crush on you too, Time.

Time: Come closer...

[They kiss.]

(The curtain falls on their silhouettes entwined.)

The Hole
A Tragedy

(Police tape around a patch of grass.)

The Hole's suicide note found on the ground: "fill me, fill me, please..."

(The grass weeps.)

High School Reunion

A Trilogy, Part I

(Two people in an empty gymnasium, TLC's "Waterfalls" plays in the background.)

You: Where is everybody?

Person with No Face: They are all dead.

You: Wanna dance?

(They dance.)

Zombie High School Reunion

A Trilogy, Part II

(A gymnasium filled with 30-somethings, TLC's "Waterfalls" plays in the background.)

Dead You: What happened to everybody?

Dead Dude from Drivers Education: They are all alive.

Dead You: Wanna eat their brains?

(They eat brains.)

High School Reunion: the Wallflower
A Trilogy, Part III

(A gymnasium full of 30-somethings, TLC's "Waterfalls" plays in the background.)

You: Where is everybody?

Girl, who is also you: We are all here.

You: Wanna dance?

(You are everyone, you all dance.)

[Fade back to see the gymnasium hurtling through space towards a black hole full of a thousand lost suns.]

Porn

A Play for the Future

You are swimming in the ocean. A bit of breeze, some sunlight on your eyelids, salt on your skin, clouds scroll by like the comments field of the sky, a wave lifts you up like a father, then puts you back down like a mother. You think of nothing or something. You are simply swimming. Everything else melts away.

All the computers and devices in the entire world are abandoned on the bottom of the ocean floor.

This is called pornography.

An Encounter with a Figure from a Dream
An American Tragedy

(You walk into a Duane Reade although you are not sure why or what you're looking for.)

(You are standing, dazed in the beauty aisle.)

You: Jesus, you scared the hell out of me!

Dream in which your Hands are Gigantic: I'm sorry.

You: What the hell are you doing here?

Dream in which your Hands are Gigantic: I followed you.

You: You can't just walk into a Duane Reade like this!

Dream in which your Hands are Gigantic: (Looks down at the ground.)

You: ...And why are you following me anyway?

Dream in which your Hands are Gigantic: Because I love you.

You: But you frighten me. You crush everything that you touch.

Dream in which your Hands are Gigantic: I was born that way, and to follow you, but something happened along the way, I fell in love with you, and it's bigger than these hands, than me, than all the gravity of the Earth...

(The manager and two Duane Reade employees approach. They grab the dream and escort it away, and as they are dragging the dream, just before it disappears, like a drugstore Eurydice, she looks back at you, sad and frightened and alone.)

Seven Sentence Fragments Enter a Bar

A Play

...even this is part of the history of forgetting enters a bar

let me be your torture boy enters a bar

I can't get "space-clit" out of my head enters a bar

Aphrodite's tricked-out soul enters a bar

throttled past the capacity to do so enters a bar

Obama's speech writer bought my book enters a bar

the face beneath the face enters a bar

The Life of a Wave 🌊

(The sea is cruel and endless and too too blue.)

Wave: Why was I born?

Wave: I was born to break. Unless!!...unless you think I may never break, I may be the exception, I may make it, I may move on past the sand, past the beach, over the dunes, across roads, through traffic, past parking lots, through fields and forests, across lawns and cities, over mountains, through deserts, to the edge of the world, through the ether, past the moon, moving through space, infinitely, forever, the wave which never breaks...

(The curtain falls. The wave takes a bow, then breaks.)

Existential Celebrity Mug Shots
A Dumbshow

(The setting is the drunk tank of existence, and a general inwardness.)

Ennui: disheveled hair, pale complexion, blood-shot eyes, ripped Joy Division shirt with mustard stain, 5 o'clock shadow, GNR earing in left ear, secret pain pouring out of pores

Malaise: double chin, Morton salt girl with umbrella tattoo on neck, Lohan-esque
fallen expression, smeared mascara, missing tooth, black eye

Neo-Kantianism: Members Only jacket (duh), tear drop tattoo, gnarly beard in what may or may not be dreads, lazy eye, lipstick kiss imprint on cheek, creepy smirk like this-was-my-plan-all-along

Nihilism: soul patch, frosted tips, spring-break hemp necklace, spectacular orange spray tan, 90s
Chicago Bulls jersey, what-you-talking-about-Willis lip snarl, middle finger to the future

New Wave
A Play

Icarus: Time is the final translator. See, I'm an entrepreneur. Lawyering up!

Simon Cowell: I'm so high right now. What do you call this stuff: "Magician's Bluff?"

Judas: It's called "Reaching for the Sun."

Icarus: Too soon, too soon.

Simon Cowell: This is some Aztec shit, I feel like Kano from Mortal Kombat is reaching into my chest for his signature heart-ripping move, holding it, wet and beating, for history to see.

Judas: Wow, Cowell... that was beautiful, like lyrics to a Judas Priest song.

Icarus: Name a dozen New Wave bands...

Simon Cowell: Judas Priest wasn't New Wave...

Judas: Joy Division, duh, The Cure, The Smiths, umm, New Order...DEVO, were they new wave?

Icarus: Isn't every wave a new wave? What would an old wave even be? It too loses life to find freedom, not failure but another form, infinitely bidding adieu adieu, it dies, yes, but what a view...

(Icarus falls...)

(Simon and Judas LOL)

Pan back to see Apollinaire reading the text to this play, the sun coming in through the window as he falls asleep with the book on his chest, and there, before the curtain falls, we see, scrawled in the margin: Blondie

Not Safe for Work

A Play Vérité

I am writing a play called NSFW

...which consists of me quitting my job in real life and leaving the city and driving directly to the ocean and living in a little house down by the sea...

The play will have no words and will last a lifetime.

HUMAN WEEK

trouble
trouble
trouble
I left
you
a note
in a field
in Carolina
to find
a new beauty
in some terrible
wind-tortured
place
words
bright like nails
a woman
walking
over a bridge
I was the water
the world's worst
carpenter
love
like nothing
else

wrap a t-shirt
around my head
and head
into battle
the kitchen
a necropolis
of knives
and pale apologies
butt-dials
to coworkers
and my blood
on the cutting-board
better believe
I do more
than spread
cream cheese
with these
civil war swords
now put down
that wine
and kneel
to the fucking king
of forgetting

my guilt fills
hot-air balloons
friends shoot
blow-darts
my direction
but I'm Rick James
high
besides it's beautiful
up here
and I am not afraid
of falling
but of being
on the ground

still don't get
the birds & the bees
real vs. metaphor
a Godzilla movie
I'd pay to see
the bees die
after the deed
but we go on
living leaving
ourselves inside
what we touch
which is why
after you
I feel like yelling
Jenga!
all the time

the genius
of Gilligan's Island
is the infinite
possibilities provided
by circumstance
imagination is an island
it takes talent
to get stranded on
I had this dream
we were walking
on a beach
beneath a ripped sky
a blue canopy
through which
it rained
red umbrellas
thus beginning
the long
and bloody
war

remember when we
searched inside
each other
after playing
Operation
I always
wondered
what shape
hole the soul
would make
it's down
to Nintendo clouds
or a person
in a panda suit

why wake
why sky
surrounded by
victories
I flop
and have
a beer
the dazzling
robot float
in no one's
parade

at the party I say
a bunch of historical shit
that never gets recorded
the world felt
as a presence
reminds me
of a field
of pool tables
due to a deficiency
my friend
thinks the ocean
is green
he is a genius
plumber
in the Times
people die
of sadness
it is beautiful
outside
yo clouds
what the fuck
is up

those two clouds
battling for rookie
of the year
a tooth tied
to a string
a field of
scarecrows on fire
a woman
with two hearts
and a poem
walking away
muttering
threats
what's in you
a nest
of *yes*

it appears
I've grown
a shark's fin
I circle
but so does
the sun
a victim of form
and fear
I must go
misunderstood
and sad
but still
human
into the cold
dark world
waiting
with a dumb
hope
for a week
dedicated
to me

tonight I break
bread
with James Wright
we share
love want(s) doubt
like a mountain
but I don't need
line breaks
to tell you
my body
will never
burst or bloom
or blossom
into anything
just shit
and piss
and pain
and die
the end

when I die
will someone please
keep me alive
in Second Life
my password
to all things
is *pipedream!*
don't forget
the exclamation
point and feel
free to bring
flowers
fuck
the sniper
in the mall
I leave
a hole
in everything

when I go toward you
it is with my whole life
like a light
beyond imagination
swinging
in a black basement
even when we don't desire it
God is ripening
night churning
like black butter
I want to wrap around you
like the head bandage
of Guillaume Apollinaire
we bleed
in black and white
like a silent film
the way we loved,
the meanings we made,
our need
the film catches fire
the audience
is left
to their devices

text me
you breathing
tumbling is some
sort of sport
if I could figure out
how to compete
I'd be a fucking champion
I say fuck a lot
but it's better than light
or stone
or somnambulant
or something
that nobody
but a poet
would say
turnstyle of sadness
how the fuck
do I get out!

history is repetition
wait
let me
begin again
history is a big egg
in midair
no wonder
this city is screwed
wish this
was a novel
so somebody
would get saved
I give up
go ghost
put on
a translucent suit
and stand
on the corner
feel
a parade
of strangers
walk
straight
through
you

meet me
at the theater
on the bottom
of the ocean
hold my
last thought
let me explain
more than
to be alone
is to be
at the center
of anything
the terrible eye
blind
becoming un
numb
please
please
take me
to where
your thinking
ends

there is always
a big adult
in the way
these days
it's you
a storm
is brewing
let's build
a moat
a boat
a flying thing
yes magic
is a trick
singing makes
no sense
beauty
is useless
do something
with it

emptiness
is necessary
for creation
fuck art
we all come
with these
exquisite holes
in our bodies
I'm convinced
one day
an animal
will crawl
out of there
we will
name it
something
religious

the sun still
spends its
fistfuls of money
and we
still waste
our lives
declaring
beauty to
the world
a whisper
inside a
cheerleader's
megaphone
go humans go!

my business
card says
penetralium inspector
developed
a not-so-secret
handshake
that's sweeping
the nation
I'm a big
big man
love
is my style
haters
go on
hating

give me
the dark
fairytales
an angel
inside me
you'd think
I'd feel it
thrashing right
give your wolves
a rest
true stories
always end
in poverty
take the one
we're trapped in
your elusive love
elaborately
engineered
impossible
to touch
a moat
of moats
and me rowing
a small man
in a small
boat

we need
a new kind
of light
that no one
will write
about
something
to erase
everything
that came
before
time
to close
your eyes
you will
now be shot
for writing
this poem

the future
is a field
of black light
time folded
in on itself
an architecture
of absence
form in
formlessness
my advice
trees
is to keep on
moving

so sing
thine army
of angels
behind me
love
may come
and go
there was
the memory
in the blood
the low call
bewilderment
and later
fulfillment
there was
the wave
that never broke
the dull blow
to the soul
your mind
riddled
with lies
the heart
with its
pretty little
holes

that last one
was called
dead bird
tattoo # 2
I too
think
of planks
not rotting
that first
bird's song
living
on
in the blood
I mean
in the ink
the mind
not a diamond
for miles

don't tell me
the young rapper
dies
at the end
don't think
I could take it
tell me something
unexpected
like a revenge shit
showing the world
a thing
or two
about shame
but all
apologies are
boring
so just shut
your mouth
and I'll
kiss it

stuck between
wife &
goddamn
I take
the road
with the most
dust
wires crackle
and hum
the grackles
disband
in a black fan
shot-through
with sun
I pretend
is you
heading
south
without a shirt
feeling lonely
but brave
because
you can't forget
the way
to
no home

suffering
isn't nearly
as cool
as I thought
but I brought
back a
few things
not unlike
flying
machines
and shored
up
some other
beliefs
like even if
I'm gone
as long
as you
are here
to read
this
I will
never
die

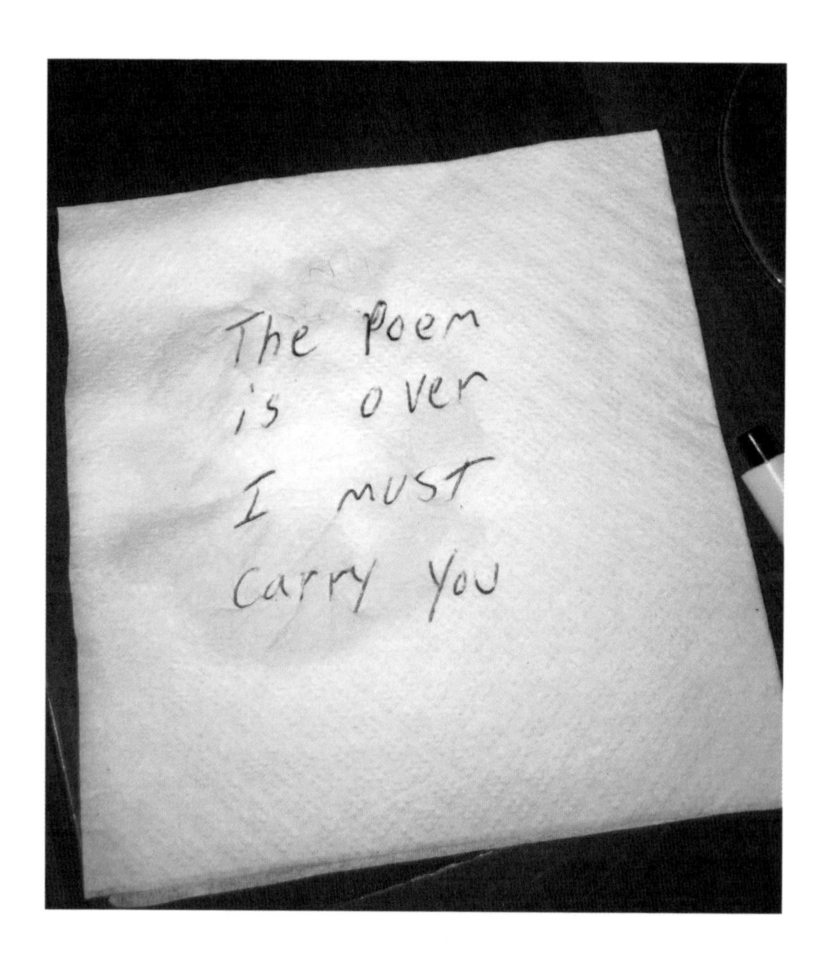
The poem
is over
I must
carry you

UNTIL THE JOY OF DEATH HITS

Is a "shrieking forest" a thing?
I feel
like it is
& I am
its king
listen
to me
sing

---

*GIF The wiggling trembling penetralium of mystery... Keats, in a letter somewhere, mentions the time Solange, in a hotel elevator, threw a flurry of ungodly haymakers & constant elbows at Jay Z... somewhere between them the secret of the universe resides.

Love, Art, Hell
share a waiting room
like a strange
efficient law firm
where we
shake the shit
out of this freedom
vending machine
nothing falls
except expectations
you fish
your hand in
and pull us
apart
like a sticky bun
or the city
with your mind
in the sense
that it's a decision
that everything
you kill
comes
back
you hear me
singing
without
a head
searching
all of hell
for you
who hold it
lovingly
in those hands
that only kill
occasionally

---

*GIF Beetlejuice and two dead people sit patiently in the bureaucratic bliss of purgatory's waiting room, as a Voodoo doctor sprinkles juju dust on Beetlejuice, shrinking his head infinitesimally.

Life is
a To-Do List
growing like a gremlin
thrown into the ocean
astounded no one's
around us
you finger scroll
the screen
a story
with no end
pixilated cities
fly into
the ground
our souls
are the post offices
of tomorrow
you text
like a teenager
I text like Dostoyevsky
we fuck
and the Internet
does not exist

---

*GIF Naked on the edge of the bed, you scramble to find the giant iPhone that controls your dreams, frantically hitting all the buttons like transcribing the most important poem of...ah, whatever.

waves of whatever
I'm waiting
to drown
in you
as if
I came
equipped
with
an emotional
flamethrower
or something
your numbness
and near
waxing detachment
is both
your superpower
and axe
in my back
so I stumble
into a field
of feels
waiting
for whatever
nature
decides
to do

---

*GIF The Grim Reaper wading out in the ocean, perpetually pummeled and drowning in waves of feels.

every emotion
is an image
the Incredible Hulk
taught us that
your face
being erased
in my mind
as survival
the way
cuttlefish
remember when
we exist
as two
disembodied smiles
that seem to say
“let’s rob a bank
together”
at the party
I try
to explain
how the ultimate
erasure
is murder
then shut up
like a genius
a bridge
burns
between
us
🌉🔥
the only art
is desire

---

*GIF A sensuous sea made of long-haired erotic gypsy fairy mermaids continually going into each other.

posting up
in the ether
becoming
color
an other
language
the false start
to love
it is
unknown
afraid
we may
relapse
into prose
we leave
one another
a mess
from a bout
with what's
intense
and what's not
welcome
to my life
as ellipsis
... now
it's your turn
to fall down
from the love
of my look
it's okay
you can stay
in this hotel
called
My Arms
as long
as you want

---

*GIF An invisible boy puts his arm around an invisible girl doubled-over in a field.

revolution: denied
transcendence: denied
I need a new debit card
and a way to say
"uncle"
in this unwilling
arm-wrestling match
with the world
what can I say
the phenomenon of nature
is coming
to a theater near you
like me
pretending to be
me
its performance
is astounding
and god knows
where it ends
life is a dress
rehearsal for
death
we nail it every time
like Kerri Strug
better bunny down
a poetics of autocorrect
won't save you
angry at anything
beautiful
we didn't create
lost
at last
in the after-
math
of
nothing
who
to such sweet lack
I surrender
guns a blazing

---

*GIF History is just God's GIF....

let me be your barcode baby
I will pay you
in falling down
OMG
Pain is my favorite song too
let's take it
next level
& smoke a j
in the shower
we are artists
because we both pretend
which makes it real
I can charge
your phone
with my mind
the strange erotics
of making do
I miss you
so much
I masturbate
with my left hand
imagine this with a city
burning behind me
hacking @ the firewall
of your desire
I give up
and have a beer
right here
at the end
of this
poem

---

*GIF Behind every bastion of capitalism is the sick ass dance moves of a bygone era.

eventually images
will eat you
alive
art
is dumb
but we do it
because
it is
(our) life
I am
the hunter
you are
the animal
that won't load
the not-world
is our audience
Do Not Touch
The Artwork

---

*GIF A painting that won't load, like the beautiful worthless bandwidth of the damned.

we work
against
ourselves
like a safety
running the wrong way
after a fumble
the number 3
in the rain
breaking
every tackle
we scream
at the screen
as if words
could make
a difference
but you're right
beside me
on your phone
and I'm afraid
what I'm trying
to say
is I suck
at this day-
to-day shit
this domestic
middle zone
so I kick it
in the afterlife
like a ghost
with a denim jacket
and bad credit
but a decent
haircut
and a few poems
in my chest
my shame
following me

like a halo
or a name
glowing
beautiful
useless

---

*GIF An old white politican-looking dude in too-tight swim trunks running to dive into a pool, only he slips and falls on his ass and bounces into a pool of pixilated light crystals.

we are on
the other side
of this life
a touch screen
(I wrote scream)
which is what
we should be
introducing
counterfeit bills
into a currency
of familiarity
I carry this cardboard
cut-out
of Miley Cyrus around
because
you never know
9/11 began the war
of images
[insert memory here]
we move
through life
gathering loss
like a moth
a winged-thing
bringing it
home
this is about
dust mutha
fucka
look
I am not a
visionary
just some dude
with a smart

phone
and
some time
to kill

---

*GIF Mutha fucking Mothra—the most glorious beautiful beast ever dreamed—fulfilling its metaphoric prophecy, beating its wings in the Technicolor dust over a helpless Godzilla on his back, so deftly declared with Apollonian grace in the movie poster's tagline "ravishing the universe for love."

imagine color
is a construct
imagine it
as music
what will fall
sounds like
a sudden gap
wedged into
the intellectual
murmur
not an argument
but a lynx
pacing around
the living room
this is
what it is
to be
with you
to be
bewildered
apart
of the
endless blur

---

*GIF When you die, there is no colorful tunnel of nature's grace to usher you into the sweet hereafter, but luckily somebody made a killer GIF of it.

reality arose
(a rose?)
from sensual
particularities
you can't smell
a rose in a poem
stupid
silence
between words
a fissure
for vividness
to eventuate
my first argument
was with a tree
which I won
I think
that cold
raw comfortlessness
that comes
from stubbornness
is from this ridiculous
thing between
my legs
the calamity
of the century
this is surely
the worst poem
ever written
which is something
anyway
now you can say
you were there

you were a part
of history
you
loser

---

*GIF The loser is a tender and underappricated animal, even the trees bend to bless them when they deign to crawl from their hovel into a world of difficult light of small awkward exchanges, poets know what I mean.

lush atmosphere
I'm making music
for you
to rest in
reverse dream
I get dizzy
check instagram
tumblr
gmail
Nothing
& Waiting For
are my gods
ellipsis (...)
that terrible
threesome
the logos
I bow
down to
my shape
is shipwreck
mainly faded
just stay
I'll read you
some early
Tomaž Šalamun
from my apartment
in this shitty city
and maybe
baby
we can make out
...
the stars
💫💫💫

---

*GIF Dante shit y'all!

so I have
a crush
on space
condescending sky
corporate blah blah blah
oblivion
blissed out
in a gold chain
whistling
in my fancy
infinity
night running
for the train
like a little bitch
I am
an analog
a dial
pointing to
TEAM PAIN →
less a man
than perpetual rain
the Nijinsky
of falling
down
disappearing
with dream-receding
speed
into this
one-man war
against torpor
a butterfly
trapped
in a conference room
this is both
the beginning
& the end
sin(g)

into oblivion
O
o
o
o
o
o
o

---

*GIF A man infinitely falling from a skyscraper, but seemingly at peace, sublime, almost swimming in the purple air, as if this was his sole purpose, to fall.

the silent film
of our perspective
is burning
the problem
is memory
(elegy)
how to live
with what
we can't keep
a flower
(a friend)
impossibly pink
(bright)
the world
in black
& white
Darkness
on the marquee
for the billionth
day in a row
but duh
this life
is on
a loop

---

*GIF Imagine Time finally succeeding in its age-old attempt to suck its own dick... in theorethical physics this phenomon is known as "the Macauley Culkin-Ryan Gosling-T-shirt continuum."

"Bury me in the barely visible"
she commands
the city
behind the city
hiding beneath
a white sheet
god playing
ghost
no one
is watching
it is beautiful
you are lost
like a white iPhone
in the snow
in this
remember-weather

---

*GIF A monk at the edge of the blue world, coming out of ice, paints a tree into existence: waiting, pinetree, frond.

fuck all limitations!
puking diamonds
floating around
inside our hangover
like a seahorse
there's that cloud again
muttering in the unionized
blue sky
of love about diffidence
password protected
watching porn
with terrible sound
dubbed like a Godzilla movie
was probably my masterpiece
worried about what
to wear or your haircut
check Instagram
& my life melts
into a black puddle
like a VHS tape
in the grass
in the end
there is no end
except forgetting
my whole life
is goddamn
I was meaning
to tell you
something

---

*GIF A nude geisha with blood-splattered face and body, barfs what seems to be the anicent art of pretending to tolerate men.

ever see
an angel
have a panic attack
it ain't pretty
feathers
everywhere
you get the picture
now replace angel
with poem
what I mean
is words matter
they ARE the poem
which means
every word
is an angel
and apparently
every angel
is terrifying
hence
the panic attacks
so slow down
baby
sit with me
let's fold time
like clean t-shirts
then when
we're through
with time
lean in
and kiss me
like every
weather ever
happening
at once

---

*GIF Robo-Pigeon: Part pigeon, part machine, all poem-angel.

I want
poems
so
simple
so
elemental
they almost
cease
to exist
the logos
of no
thing
to be
that
exact
lack

*GIF Still-life with a table of warped, bubbling, pulsing, metamorphosing, and wavy fruit, or ummm... somebody took waaaay too many mushrooms.

Joy Revision
routine
will tear us
apart
the woods
are waiting
for me
to take a bow
come home
to a letter
from Heifer United
a bill from something
I don't dare open
no emails
texts or links
will change the world
but it doesn't
stop me
from waiting for
whatever
that nothing
that's never
coming
may be
… … …
the seemingly
infinite encore
of the trees
🌲🌳🌲🌳
👏👏👏👏

---

*GIF The luminous edge of the known universe, or as far as the game developers programming extends, which like the beach in the movie *Time Bandits*, appears to extend infinitely, but when you run into the unending mirrored plane of existence, electrostatic patterns light up rippling its surface.

my desire
to destroy
art
is slightly higher
than my desire
to create it
it's not
a stretch
to say loser
is what I do
for a living
mimicking clouds
sure we have maps
but what
if they're wrong
nobody gets
this shit right
when I die
besides going HAM
on the sky
I want
to know
who will inherit
my radiant
net debt and weed-plant
sweatpants
childless
my action figure
would be
an old broke fat
afraid and alone
anxiety-riddled
sex addict
alcoholic

administrative assistant
*dope ass sweatpants
sold separately

---

*GIF The world will end in a Fanta-strewn landscape, the last fool in sweatpants, bored, logged-on to a laptop, straight lounging.

in love
we are never
so close
to rage
storms are natural
and sublime
so go ahead
duct-tape the windows
the awe of anything's
wings
is waiting

*GIF "Lazy Storm" is what Storm's mom would call her when she was a kid and wouldn't get out of bed or didn't clean her room, and well, that struck a nerve in the impressionable Storm— now she channels that when she is pissed into electricity or weather phenomenon to suit her fancy—if you've ever been outside, you've probably seen them.

a server farm
in Salt Lake City
couldn't hold
this desire
my tenderness
is infinite
like some kind of code
an IT department
would weep like Keats
at the end
of a poem
lost to a dream
it is all
for you
who
Delete All
with a finger
I fall
and you remain
in grace
a monster of unknowing
leaving me
mooing
this incessant roar
of useless love

---

*GIF An 1800-foot giant green lizard walking upright through a country farm to the chorus of the cows singing the aria of the conveniently overdubbed rapture.

Wanting vs. Waiting
the last Civil War
will be won
@ The Battle
of Why?
casualties
on either side
will sow
the future
fields
with bright
& useless
flowers
💀💀💀💀💀
🏵️🌺 🏵️🌹🌷

---

*GIF The year is 1864, a woman with black hair, her curls blowing in the wind, feels an army in her heart—it's not implicit whether they are invading or returning home.

drone porn & spiritual downloads
take up
all my memory
on this ~~sm~~art phone
sex and love come
easy and there is no
pain no
wonder
we all walk
buried in them
oblivious
to the ordinary
the astonishing horrible
saccharine real
where our bodies
do beautiful things
in defiance
of the un-ness
around them
devices are easy
to replace
besides that blackberry
a dead girl gave me
doomed to bloom
set to silence
like a black rose
in space
(my lungs)
phones don't know
dick about death
put poems
in your ears
you stupid
artless
living fools

---

*GIF A black rose in space, dripping wet with stars.

I barely graduated
Jack Spicer High
class of no numbers
ghost-hazed
4-eva summer
so so in grammar
estonish-me
etched into
my desk
desire-gnawed
2 pencils & bad magic
spelling words
longing
to be
love
a great wave
of
impossible quarterbacks
crashing
our cars
into a kind
of crepuscular music
home-
work
the radio
lodged in the back
of the throat
but O
the beautiful boys
in bathing suits
fuck this
sad ass poem
let's go
to the beach
baby

---

*GIF Lieutenant Dan, sad and despondent, stares into oblivion, pummeled by the storm of reality in the form of confetti rain.

named my hangover
Tranquilito
in a rogue attempt
at control
choked
at the audition
for my self
tenured
at the university
of doubt
responsibility
this dead horse
I call my car
my aura
"student loan"
post-Benjamin
binge meme-ing
an affair
with data
bureaucratic moon
404: timed out
still filibusting
your love
for a lifetime
requires
the sneakers
from Flubber
a field of red tape
to wade out in
waiting
for the bull
to pass through
...
the light

---

*GIF A solar eclipse caught on a VHS tape of your dead loved ones.

fingerbanging
in the library
cocaine rain
a bank on fire
a boy can dream
a celebrity crying
on the elliptical
a wheelchair
by the river bank
praying in a 96 civic
the slut-shamed stars
aggregate of light
the woods
desire
the moon in HD
a TV in the forest
a fire flickering
inside
a nightingale
sucked into an airplane
engine
poetry
an archive
of failure
in the face
of what's fucked
and what's gone
we all sing
poorly
the stitched-song
of the infinite

---

*GIF The pedestrian walk sign of an illuminated man indicating it's ok to "cross" has come to life, had a sex-change to a woman, and won't stop dancing.

tonight I will write the whitest lines
sorry space
just keep holding
that impossible pose
you guru you
sitting at my shitty
Dell is
self-flagellation
for this
sick infatuation
with the stars
shining WHY
their poor
anthropomorphic
exhaustion
of existence
I too feel
in my limbs
a long gone-
ness
the art
of pretending
to be
will be
my masterpiece
if you see me
shine
please
forgive me

---

*GIF In an otherwise empty wood-paneled room from the 70s, a lone holographic body flickers in and out of existence like an old lightbulb on the brink.

HOPE
your tattoo says
in a dead
language
I can't read
(translated by Bing)
all I know
is the want to know
is the ®ealist desire
let's get old-school
like fingerbanging
in the park
u kiss like a Goya painting
locked in a basement
the biographer of your dreams
bursts into flames 🔥
so we can see
our drugs
gracias dream-scholar
our band would be
The I Don't Knows
touring our apartment
to sold out shows
of die-hard *Nothings*
(follow them on Facebook)
our problems are not real
you are right
life IS
everything
we hail
a Death Taxi 💀🚖
from the reading
you flick the ash
from your cigarette
and smile
and the rain
rains

---

*GIF Longing and Hope hang out in a hotel room, knowing the impossibility of this moment, they smoke, trying to stop time.

the real dream
of no job
I was a masochist
I mean mascot
for a local bank
wore a bear's head
in 93 degree heat
at lunch I played
pick-up b-ball
in a furry suit
like Teen Wolf
after the game
I took off
my head
and held it
under my arm
like an astronaut
smoking a J
on the moon
with some sweaty dudes
in jorts
what happens next
pretty much
sums up
America–
a dank ass
high as shit
talking bear
tries to sell
you something
you don't need
poetry
I have found
is the best

of all
possible
hells

---

*GIF There comes a time in every person's life when you have to get high in an alley behind a bank and dance in a bear suit.

I had this idea
to write a novel
around a sentence
to live by
according to
or around
that sentence
we all crawl
towards our period
blind Ccing the future
our specific and clichéd end
this is the Introduction
to love...
the sentence was
I don't want to stand
around with you
if you don't adore me
but I broke
into fragments
like I always do
and you
move like prose
through a glass
menagerie
my hammer
it glows

---

*GIF Two turtles toss perpetual sledge hammers, virtually making it rain 20-pound mallets aimed at the protagonist's mug... as if it's not tough enough to be an overalled mustached man in a mushrooming land trying to manage worlds and time.

I dream
I am
rescuing you
from a fire
but I am
the fire
we both
burn
🔥🔥🔥
I wake and think
it is spring
we are going to die!
I decide
to walk
though the mall
naked
with a burning
sword
go down
on you
in the food court
until our audience
the sky
breaks
into thunderous
applause
this is called
Women Samurai for Survival

---

*GIF Are you a Republican?... don't turn around— you are about to be beheaded by a badass samauri who carries her own rain around with her.

the end
of images
is nigh
like
love
before
smartphones
better camel-clutch
the corporal
'cause I'm fin
da get
spiritual
so dog-ear
this entry
in my alarming
dictionary
of reformist
love
it is over
when it's over
the moon
is coming
up
I have something
to do
with that
I want
to be
the sea
constantly
crashing
going in
to my
self
up
and
down

salt
and
thrash
and
bloom
and
birth
a gif
of this

---

*GIF The wave which never breaks, a.k.a. Britney Spears

remember that game
SimCity
pretty sure I live in it
I am the secret police
of your dreams
I see you
see me
put on my plastic
hamster mask
and go to work
dismantling the rainbow
of the real
one line at a time
anything you say
can and will
be used
against you
my nightmares
are where
detectives go
to practice
between cases
disappointment is a form
of weather
and the weather
is literally everywhere
the dead
never Reply
All
somebody please
tag me
before I disappear

---

*GIF An 8-bit city confesses to the stars in an unknown video game which we often refer to as our life.

cropped out
the cops for you
then the rest
of the world
just us, love
and these lines
characters
in no play
strange stage directions
float, breathe, mean, be
if you need
the internet
we'll have
to invent
another one
maybe baby
is the most beautiful
word
the way
we say it
baby
baby
baby
I'm bankrupt
it becomes
a poem
which may be
sung
a stay of grace
we come
again and again
out of poverty

to begin
to sing
the end
this is
the end

---

*GIF Shimmer shimmer ya shimmer yam shimmer ya the stars drop the mic so the night can take it away.

ACKNOWLEDGEMENTS

In conjunction with Third Man Books, Spork Press has created an interactive multi-media chapbook website for the last section of this book *Until the Joy of Death* 💀 *Hits*. To access the animated love-pop-GIF poems, visit untilthejoyofdeathhits.com or scan here:

Thanks to the editors of the following journals and anthologies where many of these poems first appeared:

BOMB, *Hoax*, *Hyperallergic*, *Imperial Matters*, *Interrupture*, *Language Lessons*, *Pinwheel*, *Prelude*, *Sprung Formal*, *Supermachine*, *The Volta*.

Portions of this book were also published as chapbooks by Tungsten Press & Spork Press → thanks to the editors.

Some of these poems with collaborative artwork by Jon-Michael Frank were displayed in the exhibition "THE SKY IS FULL OF SHIT" for the group art show "Full Bleed: Poetry Comics" at Indy Hall in Philadelphia → thanks to the curators.

"post-police rainbow" is for Anne Boyer.

Impossible gratitude to my editor, Chet Weise, for his Spock-like-vision, encouragement, and always keeping shit real.

Thanks to Ben Swank & the Third Man Team for their belief in this book, and for their commitment to the weird, wild, and imaginative.

Thanks to my family and friends for their support, love, and help in making this book possible. Special thanks to my birds family, especially Dan Boehl, Justin Marks, Matt Rasmussen, Chris Tonelli.

Thanks to Jon-Micheal Frank for his skills and dark artwork for the PAIN poems.

Thanks to my GIF-DJ Ana Božičević for your relentless dreams, voice in my space helmet, and for creating these little infinities with me.

Most of all, to my own private language machine, my ow private beat-boxer of love, thanks to Paige Taggart, the Mothra to my Godzilla, together, ravishing the universe for love.

Some lines from this book are from or based on friends or poets I admire; some of them are H.D., Paul Celan, Iris Cushing, Bernadette Mayer, James Schuyler, & Joe Wenderoth.

Emojis are from EmojiOne, an open source.